Barbeque
Sizzling Fireside Know-How

by
Leslie Bloom

AMERICAN
★ COOKING ★
GUILD

Dedication
To David for his support and patience when sampling endless versions of the same dish; to Mom and Dad, the inspiration behind everything; to Ruth and Joe, who have remained imperturbable when faced with both grilled mussels and venison on the same menu; and to countless friends and neighbors for their tasting and proofreading skills.

Acknowledgments
—Cover photo by Burwell and Burwell

ISBN 0-942320-26-3

More Great Cookbooks!
The American Cooking Guild Collector's Series includes dozens of cookbooks on specific topics such as seafood, pasta, pizza, chicken or chocolate desserts. For a color catalog of our books, send $1.00 to us at the address below. You will receive a coupon for $1.00 off your first order.

The American Cooking Guild
6-A East Cedar Avenue
Gaithersburg, MD 20877
(301) 963-0698

Table of Contents

Introduction

Mention barbeque and it conjures up a myriad of pleasant images: casual get togethers with friends spent outdoors on sunny afternoons or balmy evenings; pungent aromas of spicy and succulent meat rising from the grill; glazed smoky-sweet delicacies, crisp and slightly charred; generous bowls of crunchy green salad, potato salad or creamy homemade coleslaw; frosty vanilla ice cream with juicy summer berries.

Cooking food directly over fire is the oldest cooking method known to man and is a favorite pastime common to many countries. For those of you lured to cooking outdoors and addicted to the grilling philosophy, this book contains various recipes to explore with your favorite foods. Once you have mastered the basic grilling techniques, investigate a variety of seasonings to develop your own flavor combinations.

Guidelines For Better Barbeques

Types of Grills

Superb grilled food begins with the use of good equipment. The two most popular types of barbeques are traditional charcoal fueled grills, heated with lump charcoal or briquettes, and the recently popular gas barbeques, which are propane fueled.

Grill Temperatures

Charcoal grills have a great range of temperatures—the trick is to catch the coals at the proper moment. The temperature is hottest and ready for searing quick-cooking foods such as steaks and hamburgers when the coals have acquired a thin coating of white ash and glow red. You should be able to hold the palm of your hand over this heat for only 2 seconds. Coals are at medium heat and good for fish and poultry when covered with a medium-thick coating of white ash. The palm test is 3 to 4 seconds. Long cooking foods such as roasts should be cooked over low heat when an abundance of white ash is present. Increase the heat for a charcoal grill by tapping the coals to remove the white ash and pushing them closer together. Lower the heat by spreading the coals apart.

The temperature in a gas grill is regulated by adjusting a temperature dial to high, medium, or low; it is quicker and easier to adjust the temperature in a gas grill. Always preheat a gas grill for 5 to 8 minutes to heat the grill rack.

A grill lid regulates temperature for both types of grills: cooking with the lid on increases the heat; raising the lid lowers the temperature. Use a high grill heat to sear meat and poultry; a medium heat for fish and seafood.

Timing
For a successful mixed barbeque, such as kabobs, choose foods that cook in about the same time. Cooking time is determined by the food's density, fragility and water content. Green peppers and zucchini pair well but cherry tomatoes and onions do not; cherry tomatoes with their thin skin and high water content cook more quickly than most other vegetables. In general vegetables such as onions, zucchini, peppers and mushrooms require 8 to 14 minutes to cook depending on their size.

Cooking time for meat varies considerably according to the type and thickness of the cut. A boned leg of lamb weighing about four and a half pounds requires an hour and a quarter of cooking on a revolving spit or 25 minutes spread flat on a grill, whereas one-inch cubes of lamb for kabobs need only 8 to 10 minutes to cook. Meat with a bone takes considerably longer to cook than boneless. Chicken breasts with the bone need 20 to 25 minutes but only 8 to 12 minutes if boned. Pork needs to be well cooked; it should test with a meat thermometer to an internal temperature of 165-170 degrees.

Cooking time for fish is partly determined by type, thickness and presence of bones. A general rule of thumb from the Canadian Fisheries Department is 10 minutes of cooking for every vertical inch of thickness. Fish fillets and steaks should be at least ¾-inch thick for barbequing to prevent drying out. The cooking times indicated above are for a covered grill; they will be slightly longer for an uncovered grill.

Testing Food: Rare, Medium or Well Done
If you forget how long food has been cooking, use the finger test to check. Press cooking meat, fish or poultry with your finger—if it feels soft and your finger almost leaves an indention in the surface, the food is rare. If the flesh is stiffer, slightly springy and offers some resistence, it is medium. Food that is well done is very firm to the touch.

Skewers
Good skewers are an important factor in successful kabob bar-bequing. Look for square or twisted metal skewers to let you easily turn food. Bamboo skewers have three advantages—they are inexpensive, disposable and are available in a variety of lengths in Oriental markets. They should be soaked in water for several hours before using to prevent them from burning when exposed to the grill's high heat.

Care of Grill and Cleaning
Brush the grill rack with oil each time you use it to lessen the chance of food sticking, or spray the rack before the grill is heated with an aerosol vegetable spray. An inexpensive 1-inch paintbrush works well to brush the grill—wash the brush with liquid detergent after each use to prevent oil from turning rancid.

Clean the grill and burn off residual food after each use by heating the barbeque for a short time when the food has been removed. Brush the rack with a stiff wire brush to loosen charred bits. *Never use commercial oven cleaner on the grill since it contains toxic substances that can be subsequently transferred to food.* If necessary, soak the grill in TSP, trisodium phosphate, a cleaning powder available in hardware stores. Once a season, to improve the efficiency of a gas grill, remove the lava rocks, clean the interior of the grill and wipe the gas pipes, being careful to keep the gas vents clear of debris. After each use, cover the cooled barbeque to slow rusting and prolong its life. A rusting propane tank can be scraped, cleaned and sprayed with rust inhibiting paint.

To Marinate, Baste or Glaze?
Marinades are usually based on an acidic liquid, oil and seasonings and serve several functions: the acid breaks down some meat fibers to tenderize meat; the oil seals in moisture and keeps food from sticking to the grill; the herbs and spices add aromatic flavor. Time for marinating ranges from 1 to 3 hours for cut-up vegetables and meat cut into thin strips to overnight for some lean, dense cuts like lamb. Large pieces of food such as roasts or whole chickens will take longer to absorb flavors than thin, small pieces of meat or fish. The longer the marinating, the stronger the flavor. Be cautious with soy based marinades—if left too long, the high salt content will draw excessive amounts of moisture from marinating food, leaving it tough and dried out.

Match marinades to food: lamb, beef and pork benefit from full-flavored marinades such as tomato based; some fish and seafood are best complemented by subtly seasoned marinades. Use either type with poultry and vegetables.

A basting sauce seasons the outside of food. Brush food often with warm basting sauce during cooking—a warmed sauce coats food more evenly than cold. A hotly debated point among barbeque fans is the use of a thin versus a thick basting sauce. A thin sauce can cause excessive dripping and cause the coals to flame and dry out food; a thick sauce can prevent too much dripping. The characteristic, slightly charred barbeque flavor we associate with outdoor cooking is only achieved by some fat and sauce dripping on the coals, and this particularly applies to gas grills. Perhaps a happy medium between the two is the answer! In any case, keep a small spray bottle filled with water beside the barbeque to extinguish flames as needed without cooling the coals too much.

A glaze has a high sugar content to produce a crisp and shiny crust on food. Brush a glaze onto food near the end of the cooking time to lessen the possibility of the sugar burning. A glaze coats warm food better than cold food—for food with a short cooking time, apply the glaze after the food has been seared and slightly warmed. Use a glaze with marinated or unmarinated food. Dry the surface of marinated food with paper towels before grilling to help the glaze coat evenly.

What to Barbeque

Often people limit their barbequing to chicken, ribs or the occasional steak. However, almost any kind of meat, poultry, fish, seafood or vegetables can be barbequed with delicious results. Grill meat, fish or poultry with or without the bone, butterflied, skewered on kabobs, or roasted on a spit. Well-marbled, tender cuts are best to use since barbequing is a dry method of cooking and toughens very lean meat. One notable exception to this rule is flank steak, which when grilled to the rare stage and sliced paper thin is tender and delicious. Surprise guests with grilled venison, duck breast, clams, oysters, monkfish, tuna, squab, Cornish game hen, or one of my favorites, a whole boned and butterflied leg of lamb.

Vegetables are one of the most versatile foods to grill: cook whole in their natural form, cut into thin slices for kabobs, or into thick wedges, chunks, halves or lengthwise steaks.

Foods to Barbeque

FISH	SEAFOOD	POULTRY	MEAT	VEGETABLES
★ cod	★ clams	★ chicken	★ beef	★ corn
★ flounder	★ mussels	★ turkey	★ lamb	★ eggplant
★ halibut	★ oysters	★ duck	★ pork	★ mushrooms
★ monkfish	★ scallops	★ Cornish hen	★ ribs	★ onions
★ salmon	★ shrimp	★ quail	★ veal	★ peppers
★ sea bass				★ potatoes
★ shark				★ squash
★ sole				★ tomatoes
★ swordfish				★ endive
★ trout				★ sweet
★ tuna				potatoes
★ turbot				

Aromatic Woods

Lend distinctive flavor to grilled foods with aromatic woods such as hickory, mesquite, alder or oak. The woods are available as chunks, nuggets or chips: chunks are 2 to 3-inch squares and can be burned alone or with charcoal; chips are thinner, about 2-inches long and ½-inch thick, and suit quick cooking on gas grills since they produce a lot of sparks when burned with charcoal; and nuggets fall between the two in size and are good for either type of grill. Place chips or nuggets in disposable 4-inch x 6-inch foil pans to prevent accumulated ash from clogging the vents in a gas grill. Soak the wood in water for 30 minutes to prolong burning and encourage proper smoking. Add them when the coals are hot and ready or after a gas grill is preheated; wait 5 minutes for the wood to begin to smoke before cooking. Lower the grill lid to intensify the smoky flavor.

Types of Aromatic Woods and Uses

Hickory: strong flavor; use with beef, pork, ribs and poultry.

Mesquite: subtle, sweet flavor; use with poultry, beef, fish, lamb, veal and seafood.

Alder: subtle, smoky flavor; use with beef and fish, especially salmon.

Oak: medium-strong flavor; use with hamburgers, poultry, fish and beef.

Do Ahead Steps

Most work involved in preparing barbequed food can be done well in advance. Make marinades and sauces 3 to 4 days ahead; clean and prepare food one day ahead; and cut up food for kabobs, marinate and skewer one day ahead. If you run out of time, let your friends personalize dinner by assembling their own kabobs!

When It's Raining!

When unexpected weather prevents you from cooking outside and you switch from the barbeque to the oven broiler, remember to preheat the broiler for at least 5 minutes before starting to cook. I find you get the fastest cooking and best air circulation by placing the food to be broiled on a cake cooling rack that has been placed on top of a cookie sheet with a low side or on a jelly roll pan. Under these circumstances, the indoor cooking time will be about the same as cooking on the grill.

Mail Order Sources for Ingredients

If you cannot locate any of the necessary ingredients in your supermarket or specialty store, you can order them from the following sources:

The Chinese Kitchen
P.O. Box 218
Stirling, NJ 07980
(201) 665-2234
Catalog free upon request.

Mexican Connection
500 E. 77th Street
New York, NY 10162
(212) 628-5374
Catalog free upon request.

Tips For Successful Barbequing

★ Use hearty seasonings in a marinade since the food to be marinated will dilute the strength.

★ Two tablespoons of marinade will marinate 4 ounces of meat, fish or poultry.

★ Use 3 times more fresh herb than dried herb, since the flavor of dried herbs is more concentrated than fresh; e.g. 1 tablespoon fresh basil = 1 teaspoon dried basil.

★ Most marinades, basting sauces and serving sauces can be stored indefinitely when refrigerated.

★ Stir marinating food to evenly distribute marinade and seasonings. Stir every hour for foods marinating up to 3 hours; every 2 hours for foods marinating longer.

★ Add fresh herbs to a serving or dipping sauce 2 hours before using to retain color.

★ When entertaining a large group, assemble kabobs one day ahead, wrap well with plastic wrap and refrigerate overnight. Disposable foil pans 16-inches x 12-inches, nested, work well. Invert the same size pan on top of the kabobs to provide extra flat storage space.

★ Small disposable foil pans work well in a gas grill for holding wood chips to keep gas vents from clogging. Nest pans for support.

★ Bring all food to room temperature before grilling to shorten cooking time.

★ If you have a large quantity of basting sauce, heat only the amount required for one meal to prevent contaminating all the sauce with the brush that has been in contact with the raw meat, fish or poultry.

★ Always brush the grill with oil to keep food from sticking. An inexpensive 1-inch paintbrush is ideal.

★ Turn food often during grilling for even cooking and to prevent burning.

★ Sear meat, poultry and vegetables for 2 minutes on each side to seal in juices; continue to turn food every 2 to 3 minutes.

★ Sear fish and seafood for 1 minute on each side and turn to prevent sticking. Continue to turn fish every 2 to 3 minutes.

★ Two tablespoons of glaze will glaze 4 to 5 ounces of meat, fish or poultry.

★ After grilling, place food on a warm platter, loosely cover with foil and keep warm in a 175° oven for 5 to 10 minutes to let meat, fish or poultry relax and juices flow from the center of the food back to the outside. When you remove them from the grill consider that these foods continue to cook a bit on standing from their residual heat.

★ If you want to grill food before guests arrive, slightly undercook it, loosely cover and let stand in a 175° oven for an hour or until ready to serve.

MARINADES

Cranberry Chili Marinade

The key to this bright and tart marinade is using both the juice and zest of a fresh lime. Try it with boneless chicken pieces for kabobs, a whole bird, or individual pieces.

½ cup whole cranberry sauce, pureed
¼ cup Heinz® chili sauce
½ teaspoon hot pepper flakes
2 teaspoons fresh lime juice
  finely grated zest of 1 lime (1 teaspoon)
½ teaspoon freshly ground black pepper
2 Tablespoons corn oil

In a bowl, mix the cranberry sauce, chili sauce, hot pepper flakes, lime juice, lime zest, pepper and oil. Coat the food with the marinade, cover and refrigerate 3 hours or overnight.

Use with: poultry.

Yield: 1 cup; **Marinates:** 2 pounds

Creamy Louisiana Marinade

Moe Cheramie, owner of Old New Orleans Seafood Market in McLean, Virginia, was the inspiration for this subtle marinade that combines traditional southern seasonings with velvety and smooth mayonnaise. The mayonnaise seals in the moisture in food to leave it juicy and tender after grilling.

½ cup mayonnaise
½ teaspoon Creole or grainy mustard
2 teaspoons fresh lemon juice
2 green onions, green and white part minced
½ teaspoon Worcestershire sauce
1 teaspoon minced fresh rosemary or ¼ teaspoon dried rosemary
1 teaspoon minced fresh basil or ¼ teaspoon dried basil
1 teaspoon minced fresh oregano or ¼ teaspoon dried oregano
½ teaspoon paprika
½ teaspoon freshly ground black pepper
¼ teaspoon cayenne
¼ teaspoon salt

In a medium-size bowl whisk the mayonnaise, mustard, lemon juice, green onions, Worcestershire sauce, rosemary, basil, oregano, paprika, pepper, cayenne and salt together. Taste and adjust seasonings. Make marinade one day ahead to blend flavors.

Coat food with marinade, cover and refrigerate for 3 hours or overnight.

Use with: fish, seafood, poultry, veal, vegetables. Great for fillets, steaks, boneless kabob chunks or chops.

Yield: ¾ cup; **Marinates:** 1½ pounds.

Fresh Herb Marinade

This is one of my favorite marinades. It is fast and easy to make, and can include any fresh herb to highlight the natural flavors of food.

> 8 Tablespoons butter, melted
> 8 Tablespoons olive oil or garlic oil (page 16)
> 2 Tablespoons minced fresh dill, tarragon, rosemary, thyme, oregano, marjoram or basil; or combination of herbs
> Kosher (coarse) salt to taste
> freshly ground black pepper to taste

In a bowl, mix the butter, olive oil and fresh herb or combination of herbs together. Generously brush food with marinade and marinate 2 hours or overnight. Just before grilling, sprinkle food with salt and pepper to taste. Brush food with unused marinade while cooking or refrigerate for future use.

Use with: beef, fish, seafood, poultry, vegetables.
Yield: ¾ cup; **Marinates:** 3 pounds.

Green Peppercorn Marinade

Green peppercorns are the unripened berries of the pepper plant. When dried, they give us the familiar whole black peppercorns we use in everyday cooking. Green peppercorns have a soft texture and a sharp and tangy flavor. Look for them in specialty markets.

> 1 ½ Tablespoons green peppercorns, drained
> ½ teaspoon salt
> ¾ cup crème fraîche or sour cream
> 2 Tablespoons white wine vinegar

In a mortar or small bowl, mash the green peppercorns with the salt to form a paste. Gradually mix in the crème fraîche and vinegar. Coat food with marinade and marinate 4 hours or refrigerate overnight.

Use with: poultry, beef, fish, vegetables.
Yield: 1 cup; **Marinates:** 2 pounds.

Ginger Hoisin Marinade

This recipe was inspired by my friend, Ginger Lew's recipe for Hoisin marinade. Hoisin sauce or Chinese barbeque sauce is a great base for a variety of seasonings; use it to build a marinade, a basting sauce or a glaze.

½ cup + 2 Tablespoons Hoisin sauce
3 large cloves garlic, minced
1 Tablespoon minced fresh ginger
2 teaspoons cumin
3 Tablespoons rice vinegar
3 Tablespoons medium dry sherry
4 Tablespoons corn oil
¼ teaspoon freshly ground black pepper

In a bowl, whisk the Hoisin, garlic, ginger, cumin, rice vinegar, sherry, corn oil and pepper together. Coat food and marinate 3 hours or refrigerate overnight, stirring occasionally. The marinade refrigerates indefinitely.

Use with: ribs, lamb, poultry, pork, vegetables.

Note: Hoisin sauce is made with soy beans, vinegar, sugar, garlic, sesame seeds, water, flour, salt, chili and spices. It is available in any Oriental market and most gourmet stores.

Yield: 1 ½ cups; **Marinates:** 5 pounds.

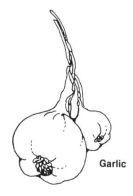

Garlic

Garlic Oil

For centuries garlic has been used to treat everything from earaches, poison ivy and insomnia to fainting and convulsions! If you are in good health but a professed garlic lover, you will find many uses for this homemade garlic oil.

10 large garlic cloves, peeled
2 cups olive oil

Smash garlic cloves lightly with the wide part of a French knife to permit more garlic flavor to penetrate the oil. Place the cloves in the bottom of a pint jar, pour oil over top and cover. Let stand at room temperature for three days before using, shaking occasionally.

Taste oil and remove garlic. For a stronger garlic flavor, let garlic stand in oil one or two more days. (Reserve garlic, cover and refrigerate, and use as you would fresh garlic.) Store remaining garlic oil in a cool dark place, and refrigerate if not using within three weeks. The oil will keep refrigerated for two months.

Brush food with garlic oil and marinate for three hours or overnight. Sprinkle food with Kosher (coarse) salt and freshly ground black pepper just before grilling. Brush food with garlic oil while grilling if desired.

Use with: beef, pork, fish, seafood, poultry, vegetables, hot dogs, hamburgers.

Other uses: Great on shrimp or clams in the shell; team garlic oil with melted butter and fresh lemon to use as a dipping sauce for seafood; brush onto thick slices of French bread and grill until crisp.

Yield: 2 cups.

Teriyaki Marinade

This traditional Oriental marinade takes first place as Creative Caterer's most popular. Over the past five years we've made 1,000 pounds of Teriyaki Chicken Tips using this marinade.

½ cup medium sweet sherry
½ cup soy sauce
¼ cup packed brown sugar
2 garlic cloves, smashed
½ teaspoon freshly ground black pepper
¼ cup corn oil

In a medium-size saucepan bring the sherry and soy sauce to a boil. Stir in the brown sugar and simmer covered over low heat for 5 minutes to dissolve the sugar. Remove from the heat and stir in the garlic, pepper and corn oil. Cool before using.

Marinate food for 3 hours or up to 12 hours, stirring occasionally. Do not marinate overnight since the high salt content will draw excess moisture from meat and toughen it. Drain food and discard used marinade since it contains meat juices and will spoil. Any unused marinade will keep refrigerated indefinitely.

Use with: poultry, pork, beef, fish, vegetables, lamb.

Hint: Teriyaki Chicken Tips—Cut skinless boned breasts into 15 finger-size strips, 2-inches x ½-inch. Marinate, sprinkle with sesame seeds and grill for 4 minutes, turning once. Serve warm or at room temperature.

Yield: 1 ½ cups; **Marinates:** 2 pounds.

BASTING SAUCES

Mustard Crème Fraîche Basting Sauce

For a truly elegant meal, grill fresh salmon and baste with a luxurious crème fraîche sauce. Crème fraîche is a cultured dairy product similar to sour cream but extremely thick; it will not curdle when exposed to high heat.

>   grated zest of 1 lemon
> 2 Tablespoons meaux moutarde (grainy mustard)
> ½ teaspoon salt
> ½ cup crème fraîche *
>   *Available in specialty markets (or substitute sour cream for the crème fraîche).*

In a bowl, whisk the lemon zest, mustard, salt and crème fraîche together. Use warm to baste food while grilling, or use as a marinade. This sauce can be kept refrigerated for up to three weeks.

Use with: fish, seafood, veal, pork, vegetables.

Hint: Use salmon and fish in cubes for kabobs, whole in fillets or as steaks.

Yield: ¾ cup; **Bastes:** 1½ pounds.

Lemon Cilantro Basting Sauce

Cilantro, the Spanish translation of coriander, is one of my favorite herbs. It looks like parsley but has long stems and a distinctive and pungent earthy lemon taste. Cilantro is one of the world's most used herbs and is a primary ingredient in the cooking of the Middle East, China, Spain, Latin America and Mexico. Look for it in Spanish and Oriental markets.

2 Tablespoons butter, melted
6 Tablespoons fresh lemon juice
1 teaspoon grated lemon zest
2 Tablespoons cold water
2 Tablespoons Thai fish sauce *
¼ to ½ teaspoon Sambal Oelek (ground chili paste) *
¼ teaspoon white pepper
¼ cup minced fresh cilantro leaves
    * Available in Oriental markets.

In a bowl, mix the butter, lemon juice, lemon zest, water, Thai fish sauce, Sambal Oelek, white pepper and cilantro. Use warm to baste food while grilling.

Use with: seafood, fish, poultry.

Hint: Clams in the shell are great with the lemon cilantro basting sauce. Grill them directly over the heat or in a foil pan to retain juices. Baste the clams when the shells begin to open after about 5 minutes and continue cooking and basting for 10 to 15 minutes. (Discard any clams that do not open.) Add any leftover sauce to the baking pan and taste. If clam juices are too salty, add water. Warm sauce and serve clams with thick crusty slices of grilled French bread.

Yield: ¾ cup; **Bastes:** 1½ pounds or 18 cherrystone clams in shell.

Four Seasons Herb Sauce

This vibrant and piquant sauce is similar to pesto, the Italian sauce made with fresh basil. Even in mid-winter, the herb sauce is as fresh and green as spring and is ideal for year round barbequing.

> 1 bunch fresh parsley, leaves picked from stems
> 1 bunch fresh watercress, leaves picked from stems
> 3 garlic cloves, peeled
> 4 green onions, coarsely chopped
> 1 Tablespoon Dijon mustard
> ½ to 1 teaspoon salt
> ½ to 1 teaspoon freshly ground black pepper
> 2 Tablespoons dried basil or oregano
> 1¼ to 1½ cups olive oil

Wash the parsley and watercress leaves in a strainer; drain and spread leaves in single layers on clean dish towels. Roll towels jellyroll style and squeeze to dry leaves. The sauce can be made by hand or in the food processor. To make by hand, mince the garlic, parsley, watercress and green onions. Combine the minced ingredients, mustard, salt, pepper and basil in a medium-size bowl and slowly whisk in the olive oil.

To make in a food processor, fit the processor with the steel blade and mince the garlic. Repeat with the parsley, watercress, green onions, mustard, salt, pepper and basil. With the machine running slowly add the olive oil until it is "brushing" consistency. Taste and adjust seasonings.

Store the sauce in a glass jar and press plastic wrap directly on top of the sauce to lessen discoloration. Cover and refrigerate up to 3 weeks, or freeze in small batches for easy use. Heat marinade on low heat before using. Sear food, and brush with sauce during cooking, turning food often for even cooking.

Use with: poultry, fish, seafood, vegetables.

Yield: 2½ cups; **Bastes:** 4 to 6 pounds.

Mom's Basic BBQ Sauce

Growing up in Northern Ontario, there was always a jar of Mom's Basic BBQ Sauce in the refrigerator—and not only in the summertime. In the winter, my father would don his heavy parka, sweep the snow off the grill, and barbeque our traditional Friday night steak, with Mom's sauce of course!

Everyone has their favorite barbeque sauce and this one is my family's favorite. I usually make 2 quarts of Mom's sauce at a time —some to have on hand for cooking and extra to give as gifts to barbeque loving friends!

½ cup packed brown sugar
⅓ cup cider vinegar
½ cup Worcestershire sauce
1 cup strong coffee
1½ cups ketchup
½ cup corn oil

In a medium saucepan off the heat, mix the brown sugar, cider vinegar, Worcestershire sauce and coffee. Whisk in the ketchup and corn oil. Bring the sauce to a boil and simmer uncovered for 5 minutes to blend flavors. Cool and store refrigerated indefinitely; warm the sauce before using to baste.

Use with: ribs, hot dogs, hamburgers, beef, fish, seafood, pork, poultry, lamb.

Note: This barbeque sauce serves as a basis for the variations that follow.

Yield: 4 cups; **Bastes:** a lot!

Mom's BBQ Sauce Variations

It's easy and fun to adapt a familiar recipe with the extensive selection of ethnic ingredients on grocers' shelves today. Puree peppers or garlic and add to the basic sauce with a variety of herbs and spices to create your own sauce from afar. Use any of the variations (recipes follow) to marinate meat, poultry, seafood or vegetables.

Five Pepper Basting Sauce

Paul Prudhomme has greatly popularized the use of several types of pepper in one dish. He feels the combination will fill your mouth with a gradual explosion of tastes as the peppers contact different parts of your tongue—black pepper at the tip of the tongue, white pepper in the middle and cayenne at the back! In case you didn't know, paprika is ground from dried chili peppers.

½ *teaspoon salt*
2 *Tablespoons green peppercorns, drained and dried on paper towels*
1 *teaspoon freshly ground black pepper*
½ *teaspoon white pepper*
½ *teaspoon paprika*
good pinch cayenne
1 *Tablespoon fresh lemon juice*
1 *cup Mom's Basic BBQ sauce or ¼ recipe (page 21)*

Mash the salt, green peppercorns, black pepper, white pepper, paprika and cayenne together. Put into a small saucepan and stir in the lemon juice and basic sauce. Bring to a boil and simmer covered for 5 minutes to blend flavors, or microwave for 2 minutes. Taste and adjust seasonings. This sauce can be refrigerated indefinitely; warm before using. Use this sauce as a marinade if desired.

Use with: ribs, beef, poultry, pork, hamburgers, lamb, fish.

Yield: 1 cup; **Bastes:** 2 pounds.

Ancho Chili BBQ Sauce

The Ancho chili is a commonly used chili in Mexico. It is actually the Poblano chili, ripened and dried. The average Ancho chili is 4-inches long and 3-inches wide, and is triangular in shape; the skin is wrinkled and dark reddish brown in color. The Ancho is one of the milder chilies and has a sweet earthy taste. You can find these chilies in Spanish markets.

> 4 *dried Ancho chilies*
> 1 *Tablespoon minced garlic*
> ½ *teaspoon ground cloves*
> 1 *teaspoon ground cumin*
> 1 *teaspoon white pepper*
> 2 *teaspoons salt*
> 1 *Tablespoon freshly ground black pepper*
> 2 *cups Mom's Basic BBQ Sauce or ½ recipe (page 21)*

Remove the stem and seeds from the Ancho chilies. Place chilies in a small pot and pour water over them to just cover. Bring to a boil and simmer covered for 5 minutes. Let stand off the heat for 5 minutes until chilies are softened. Drain, reserving liquid to poach chicken, cook pasta, etc.

In the work bowl of a food processor, with the steel blade puree the chilies, garlic, cloves, cumin, white pepper, salt and black pepper for 10 seconds to form a paste, scraping the bowl as necessary. With the machine running, add the basic BBQ sauce until the sauce is pureed and smooth. (If a food processor is not available, use a mortar and pestle or a blender.)

In a saucepan, bring the sauce to a boil and simmer covered for 5 minutes to blend flavors or microwave for 3 minutes. This sauce can be refrigerated indefinitely; heat before using to baste.

Use with: ribs, hot dogs, hamburgers, pork, poultry, fish. Great with boneless cubed chicken or pork, marinated and skewered for kabobs. Serve with a crunchy Taco salad.

Yield: 2½ cups: **Bastes:** 5 pounds.

Cajun Basting Sauce

When you want to pull out all the stops, serve "A Sure Thing!" Butterflied and skewered jumbo shrimp, basted with Cajun sauce and grilled until crisp and juicy are one of the most popular appetizers of Creative Caterers. Perfect for a cocktail party or as part of a New Orlean's buffet.

> 2 cups Mom's Basic BBQ sauce or ½ recipe (page 21)
> 2 teaspoons minced garlic
> 1 teaspoon dried oregano
> 1 teaspoon dried basil
> 2 teaspoons crushed dried rosemary leaves
> 2 bay leaves, crushed
> 1 Tablespoon paprika
> ½ to 1 teaspoon cayenne
> 1 Tablespoon freshly ground black pepper
> 1 teaspoon salt
> 1 Tablespoon fresh lemon juice

In a small saucepan, mix the basic sauce with the garlic, oregano, basil, rosemary, bay leaves, paprika, cayenne, black pepper, salt and lemon juice. Bring the sauce to a boil and simmer covered for 5 minutes to blend flavors or microwave for 3 minutes. Taste and adjust seasonings. This sauce can be refrigerated indefinitely; warm before using to baste. Sauce can be used as a marinade also.

Use with: ribs, seafood, fish, poultry, hamburgers, hot dogs, pork.

Yield: 2 cups; **Bastes:** 4 pounds.

Holiday Basting Sauce

Angostura bitters impart character to this tart and sweet basting sauce. Bitters are a combination of herbs, vegetables and alcohol and come from Angostura, a Venezuelan city now called Cuidad Bolivar after a native son who liberated his country from Spain in 1821.

> ½ cup whole berry cranberry sauce
> 1 Tablespoon freshly squeezed orange juice
>   grated rind of 1 orange, about 1 Tablespoon
> ½ teaspoon freshly ground black pepper
> 3-4 dashes Angostura bitters
>   dash Tabasco®
> 1 cup Mom's Basic BBQ Sauce or ¼ recipe (page 21)

In the work bowl of the food processor with the steel blade, or in a blender, puree the cranberry sauce, orange juice, orange rind, pepper, bitters and Tabasco for 10 seconds, scraping the sides as necessary. With the machine running add the basic sauce and puree until smooth.

In a saucepan, bring the sauce to a boil and simmer covered for 5 minutes to blend flavors or microwave for 3 minutes. Taste and adjust seasonings. This sauce can be refrigerated indefinitely; warm sauce before using to baste. Use sauce as a marinade also.

Use with: poultry, pork.

Yield: 1½ cups; **Bastes:** 3 pounds.

Pepper

GLAZES

A glaze combines three of my favorite tastes—spicy, tart and sweet—and adds a lustrous crisp crust to grilled meat and fish. A glaze will keep indefinitely when covered and refrigerated. Use glazes over a medium hot fire to brown sugar; too cool a fire will not caramelize the sugar which is needed to produce a shiny crust, and too hot a fire will burn the outside.

Honey Mustard Glaze

2 Tablespoons soy sauce
2 Tablespoons dry mustard
1 Tablespoon vinegar
6 Tablespoons honey

In a bowl, stir the soy sauce into the mustard to make a smooth paste. Add the vinegar and honey and stir until blended. Warm glaze before using. Brush glaze onto food during last 15 minutes of cooking. Baste and turn food every 1 to 2 minutes for kabobs, and every 2 to 3 minutes for larger pieces such as ribs.

Use with: ribs, poultry, pork, salmon.

Yield: ¾ cup; **Glazes:** 1½ pounds of food.

Maple Syrup Glaze

In the spring we use to tap our maple tree to collect the sap and then boil it to produce an extremely small amount of golden maple syrup. My family tells a story that when I was in very early grade school, I insisted that my teacher must have the syrup—much to the frustration of my weary parents, who literally stood for hours stirring the sap in a large pot over a hot stove!

> 1 Tablespoon dry mustard
> 1 Tablespoon cornstarch
> 1 teaspoon cumin
> ⅛ teaspoon cloves
> ⅛ teaspoon allspice
> ⅛ teaspoon mace
>   grated rind of 1 orange (1 Tablespoon zest)
> 1 Tablespoon orange juice
> 1 Tablespoon white vinegar
> 8 Tablespoons maple syrup

In a bowl, mix the dry mustard, cornstarch, cumin, cloves, allspice, mace and orange rind. Stir in the orange juice and vinegar to make a paste. Gradually mix in the maple syrup. In a small saucepan bring the glaze to a boil and simmer for 2 to 3 minutes until thickened and shiny. Use warm or reheat before using.

Brush glaze onto food during last 15 minutes of cooking. Baste and turn food every 1 to 2 minutes for kabobs and every 2 to 3 minutes for larger pieces such as chops.

Use with: ribs, pork, poultry, ham, veal.

Yield: ½ cup; **Glazes:** 1 pound of food.

Yakidare Glaze

Yaki = grilled; dare = sauce in Japanese. The Japanese brush a soy Mirin sauce on Yakitori grilled chicken and on sushi with smoked eel to impart the traditional sweet and salty taste they love. Mirin is a sweet cooking wine made from glutinous rice that is used in Japanese cooking. Look for Mirin without the prefix "agi"—these have seasonings added to them. You can find Mirin in Japanese or Oriental grocery stores.

> *1 Tablespoon sugar*
> *½ cup soy sauce*
> *1 cup Mirin*

In a wide-mouth saucepan mix the sugar, soy sauce and Mirin. Bring to a boil, reduce heat to medium and gently boil for 5 to 7 minutes or until reduced to ¾ cup and syrupy, stirring often.

Use glaze at room temperature. Brush glaze onto food during last 10 minutes of cooking. Baste and turn food every 1 to 2 minutes for kabobs and every 2 to 3 minutes for larger pieces such as chicken breasts.

Use with: poultry, pork, lamb, eel, salmon, seafood, swordfish, whitefish, vegetables.

Wildcat Inn Grilled Chicken: Grill boneless chicken breasts, baste liberally with Yakidare Glaze and sprinkle with sesame seeds. Grill big sesame seed buns, spread with Mustard Sauce (page 34) and sandwich chicken between buns. Great for a quick supper!

Glazed Belgian Endive: Cut endive in half lengthwise, leaving core intact to hold leaves together. Brush endive with olive oil and grill over medium high heat for 2 minutes each side. Contiue to cook endive for 4 to 5 minutes, brushing with Yakidare Glaze and turning often. Sprinkle with caraway seeds and serve endive warm or at room temperature.

Yield: ¾ cups; **Glazes:** 1½ pounds of food.

Sweet and Spicy Hoison Glaze

Sambal Oelek is a deep rust red paste of ground fresh chilies, salt and vinegar that has a fiery and searing taste. It is commonly used in Oriental, Thai and Indonesian cuisines. Sambal Oelek can be stored indefinitely in a non-corrosive container at room temperature. Be careful not to confuse it with chili paste which contains other seasonings including garlic and soy beans. Sambel Oelek and Hoisin sauces are available in Oriental markets.

$\frac{1}{3}$ cup chili sauce (Heinz®)
$\frac{1}{4}$ cup pureed apricot preserves
$\frac{1}{4}$ cup Hoisin sauce
1 Tablespoon + 1 teaspoon cider vinegar
2 teaspoons Sambal Oelek (ground chili paste)
2 garlic cloves, minced
$\frac{1}{4}$ cup corn oil

In a small bowl, combine the chili sauce, apricot preserves, Hoisin sauce, cider vinegar, Sambal Oelek, garlic and corn oil until blended.

Warm glaze before using. Brush glaze onto food during last 15 minutes of cooking. Baste and turn food every 1 to 2 minutes for kabobs and every 2 to 3 minutes for larger pieces such as ribs.

Use with: ribs, pork, poultry.

Yield: 1 cup; **Glazes:** 2 pounds of food.

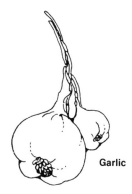

Garlic

SERVING & DIPPING SAUCES

Be prepared to find guests in the kitchen looking for a thick slice of French bread to finish up any of these leftover sauces. You can spoon a little sauce on your plate and dip meat into it...pour it over vegetables...use it as a dip. Let your imagination be your guide when serving these versatile sauces.

Ginger Plum Sauce

An unusual sweet and sour sauce that both kids and adults adore! The elusive flavors of this sauce result from a trio of sweet fruit preserves combined with tart chili sauce, heady garlic and pungent ginger. Make a large batch to have on hand; it refrigerates for months and goes with almost any grilled food.

> 1 cup Chinese plum sauce, pureed*
> 2 teaspoons dry mustard
> 1 cup mango chutney, pureed
> 1 cup apricot preserves, pureed
> ½ cup chili sauce (Heinz®)
> 1 Tablespoon peeled, minced ginger
> 8 garlic cloves, peeled, minced
> *Available in Oriental markets.

Mix two tablespoons of the plum sauce with the dry mustard to form a smooth paste. Stir in the remaining plum sauce, mango chutney, apricot preserves, chili sauce, ginger and garlic. Taste and adjust seasonings. Cover and refrigerate.

Use with: poultry, beef, pork, veal, lamb, shrimp.

Yield: about 4 cups; **Serves:** lots!

Japanese Dipping Sauce

You may be familiar with Wasabi as the fiery green paste that accompanies sushi in a Japanese restaurant. Wasabi actually is fresh green horseradish root that is dehydrated into a powder and sold in tins in this country. To use, mix with water to form a paste and let stand for 5 minutes to develop the intense flavor. Wasabi should be used within 3 hours of mixing since its hotness disappears quickly.

2 teaspoons water
4 teaspoons Wasabi powder*
6 Tablespoons soy sauce
4 Tablespoons rice vinegar*
2 Tablespoons + 2 teaspoons fresh lemon juice
2 green onions, green and white part minced
   *Available in Oriental or Japanese markets.

In a small bowl, stir the water into the Wasabi powder to form a heavy paste. Cover and let stand for 5 minutes. Whisk in the soy sauce, rice vinegar and lemon juice. Add the green onions just before serving. To use, serve sauce in a separate bowl for each guest and dip food into sauce.

Use with: sliced flank steak, seafood, firm fleshed white fish, chicken, lamb.

Yield: ¾ cup; **Serves:** 2 to 3.

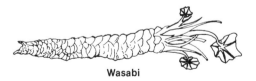

Wasabi

Roasted Red Pepper Velvet

The smoky taste of this sauce comes from roasting fresh red peppers on the grill. Grill whole peppers over medium high heat until the skin blisters and chars, turning peppers every 1 to 2 minutes to evenly cook. Place the peppers in a pot, cover and let stand off the heat for 10 minutes until the skin peels off with a small sharp knife.

    1½ cups corn oil
     1 egg, room temperature
     2 Tablespoons fresh lemon juice
     1 teaspoon red wine vinegar
    1½ Tablespoons Dijon mustard
     1 teaspoon salt
     ½ teaspoon freshly ground black pepper
     6 or more dashes Tabasco® sauce
     2 large red peppers, roasted, peeled, seeded, coarsely
        chopped

The sauce can be made in the food processor or by hand. In the workbowl of a food processor, with the steel blade process 3 tablespoons corn oil with egg, lemon juice, vinegar, mustard, salt, pepper and Tabasco for 5 seconds until mixed. With machine running, slowly add remaining oil through the feed tube until sauce thickens to form mayonnaise. Add the peppers with the machine off, then process with several on/off turns until the peppers are coarsely chopped.

To make the sauce by hand, whisk 3 tablespoons corn oil with egg, lemon juice, vinegar, mustard, salt, pepper and Tabasco until mixed. Slowly drizzle in the oil, whisking constantly to form a mayonnaise. Chop the peppers into ¼-inch dice, and stir into the sauce. Taste and adjust seasonings. The sauce can be refrigerated up to a week.

Use with: vegetables, fish, seafood, poultry, veal.

Note: You can substitute ½ cup drained, dried (on paper towels), and coarsely chopped bottled roasted peppers or pimento for the red peppers.

Yield: 2 cups; **Serves:** 12.

Scandinavian Chive Cream

This savory golden sauce often accompanies a chunky Scandinavian herring, apple and beet salad on a buffet table. It is the perfect complement to simple grilled foods.

3 hard cooked egg yolks
1 Tablespoon Dijon mustard
1 Tablespoon white wine vinegar
½ teaspoon salt
½ teaspoon white pepper
¼ cup corn oil
2 Tablespoons whipping cream
5 Tablespoons minced fresh chives

In a small bowl, mash the egg yolks with the Dijon mustard to form a smooth paste. Stir in the vinegar, salt and pepper. Slowly whisk in the oil. Whisk in the cream one tablespoon at a time until the sauce is the consistency of heavy cream. Stir in the chives just before serving. Taste and adjust seasonings. Refrigerate sauce up to one week. Serve sauce at room temperature.

Use with: fish, seafood, poultry, pork, veal.

Yield: 1 cup; **Serves:** 6 to 8.

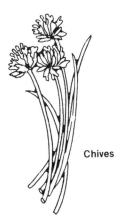

Chives

My Favorite Mustard Sauce

This creamy and piquant sauce is great with any grilled food —it's also easy to make, and will keep forever, refrigerated.

   ½ cup + 2 Tablespoons mayonnaise
   ¼ cup + 2 Tablespoons Dijon mustard
   ½ to 1 teaspoon Worcestershire sauce
   8 to 10 dashes Tabasco®

Whisk the mayonnaise, mustard, Worcestershire sauce and Tabasco together. Taste and adjust seasonings.
Use with: poultry, beef, pork, seafood, fish, vegetables.
Yield: 1 cup; **Serves:** 8.

Mustard

ENTRÉES

Tarragon Salmon Kabobs with Sour Cream Sauce

This is one of the prettiest and easiest dishes I know. The pale pink salmon flesh complements the fire engine red peppers and forest green zucchini.

Sour Cream Sauce
- ½ cup sour cream
- ¼ cup plain flavored yogurt
- ¼ teaspoon salt
- ¼ teaspoon freshly ground black pepper
- 1 Tablespoon white wine vinegar
- 3 Tablespoons minced fresh tarragon or 1 teaspoon dried tarragon

Tarragon Salmon Kabobs
- 4 Tablespoons olive oil
- 2 Tablespoons fresh lemon juice
- 2 Tablespoons minced fresh tarragon or 2 teaspoons dried tarragon
- 1¾ pounds salmon fillet, skinned, boned, cut into 1-inch cubes
- 1 red pepper, seeded, cut into 1-inch cubes
- 1 zucchini, sliced into ⅛-inch circles
- 16 mushrooms, cleaned
- ½ to 1 teaspoon Kosher (coarse) salt
- ¼ to ½ teaspoon freshly ground black pepper

To prepare the sauce, mix the sour cream, yogurt, salt, pepper, vinegar and tarragon. Cover and refrigerate.

Continued On Next Page

To prepare the marinade, mix the olive oil, lemon juice and tarragon.

Alternate the salmon, red pepper, zucchini and mushrooms on skewers, allowing 2 skewers per person. Completely brush the kabobs with the olive oil marinade, cover and refrigerate until ready to grill. Assemble one day ahead if desired. Sprinkle with salt and pepper just before grilling.

Brush grill with oil, and grill kabobs over medium heat for 6 to 8 minutes, turning every 2 minutes. Brush with leftover olive oil mixture from pan, if desired. Do not overcook or salmon will dry out. Let stand loosely covered for 5 minutes before serving.

Serve the sour cream sauce in a separate bowl and spoon over kabobs.

Hint: The marinade and sour cream sauce work well with sea bass, red snapper, cod, scallops, shrimp, swordfish, trout or mahi mahi.

Serves: 4.

Sesame Glazed Sole Strips

Perfect with marinated herbed cucumber and tomato slices, and an Oriental rice salad studded with snow peas, water chestnuts, scallions and pickled ginger. Present these delicately flavored kabobs as an appetizer on short bamboo skewers or as a light lunch with mustard sauce.

⅓ *cup soy sauce*
⅔ *cup Aji-Mirin, sweet cooking rice wine**
4 *teaspoons sugar*
2 *Tablespoons rice vinegar**
1½ *pounds skinned sole, turbot or flounder fillet*
3 *Tablespoons toasted sesame seeds or black sesame seeds*
2 *to 3 Tablespoons minced fresh parsley*
*Available at Oriental and Japanese markets.

To prepare the glaze, in a wide-mouthed 9-inch skillet, mix the soy sauce, Mirin and sugar. Boil uncovered on medium-high heat for 4 to 5 minutes, stirring constantly until syrupy. Add the vinegar and boil 1 minute; there should be about ½ cup glaze. Let stand at room temperature until ready to use.

Cut a pencil thin center piece from the fish fillet if bony. Cut fish into strips 1½-inches wide and 5-inches long. If using flounder, gently pound each strip between dampened plastic wrap to flatten. Thread fish onto skewers, allowing 2 skewers per person. Cover and refrigerate.

Brush grill with oil to prevent fish from sticking. Sear strips for 3 minutes over medium high heat, turning once. Brush with glaze and grill strips for 3 to 4 more minutes, basting often. Sprinkle with sesame seeds near end of cooking. Serve strips warm, sprinkled with fresh parsley.

Serves: 4.

Flank Steak with Meaux Moutarde

Meaux moutarde is a combination of crushed whole and ground black mustard seeds that has a crunchy texture and a nutty hot flavor.

1½ pounds flank steak
2 Tablespoons meaux moutarde or grainy mustard
2 Tablespoons white wine vinegar
2 Tablespoons dry white vermouth
4 teaspoons minced fresh rosemary or 1 ½ teaspoons dried crushed rosemary leaves
¼ teaspoon white pepper
½ cup corn oil

Trim the flank steak and place in a flat non-corrosive pan. Whisk the meaux moutarde, vinegar, vermouth, rosemary, pepper and oil together and pour over the steak. Cover and refrigerate overnight, turning several times.

Drain meat, pat dry with paper towels and sear steak on high heat for 2 minutes per side. Cook steak for a total of 2 to 3 minutes more and baste carefully with the warm marinade; this marinade flames easily.

Let steak rest for 5 to 7 minutes loosely covered on a warm platter. Slice very thin across the grain and serve with accumulated pan juices.

Hint: Grilled mushroom kabobs and Swedish potatoes make good accompaniments to this steak.

Serves: 4.

Monkfish with Jalapeño Peppers and Cilantro

Monkfish has snow white and succulent, firm flesh that adapts to hearty seasonings; its boneless fillet looks like a white beef tenderloin. For an extra special flavor, grill monkfish over fragrant wood.

  1 cup Heinz® chili sauce
  1 Tablespoon cider vinegar
  3 green onions, green and white part minced
  1½ teaspoons minced fresh jalapeño peppers,
      seeds removed*
  ¼ teaspoon chili powder
  ¼ teaspoon freshly ground black pepper
  1½ teaspoon liquid smoke **
  3 Tablespoons minced fresh cilantro *
  1½ pounds monkfish fillet
  1 medium zucchini, sliced into ⅛-inch circles, about 35
  8 mushrooms, cleaned
  1 red onion, skinned, quartered, separated
      *Available in Spanish and Oriental markets.
      **Liquid smoke is a natural product made of condensed
      vapor from a smoke house.

To prepare the marinade, mix the chili sauce, vinegar, green onions, jalapeño peppers, chili powder, pepper, liquid smoke and cilantro. Let stand 4 hours before using to develop flavors. The marinade is strong since the food will dilute it.

Cut monkfish into 1-inch x 1½-inch cubes and marinate for 4 hours or refrigerate overnight, stirring occasionally. Add the vegetables 2 hours before skewering.

Alternate the fish and vegetables on skewers, allowing 2 skewers per person. Assemble skewers one day ahead if desired. Bring to room temperature before cooking. Grill kabobs over medium heat for 8 to 10 minutes, turning every 2 minutes. Do not overcook or fish will get tough. Let stand, loosely covered in a warm place for 5 minutes before serving.

Hint: Great served with crisp golden home fries and a red leaf lettuce salad with chunks of velvety avocado.

Serves: 4.

Tuna Steaks with Juniper Orange Marinade

The juniper berry, a favorite seasoning of the Pacific Northwest Indians and the primary flavoring agent that gives gin its distinctive taste, provides an intriguing balance to the rich flavor and dense texture of fresh tuna. Look for the berries in health food stores.

½ cup dry red wine, such as Côtes du Rhône
10 juniper berries, smashed
1 teaspoon minced orange zest
2 Tablespoons orange juice
½ teaspoon dried thyme
2 teaspoons minced garlic
¼ teaspoon freshly ground black pepper
3 Tablespoons olive oil
1¾ to 2 pounds center cut tuna steak (or 1 ½ pounds of boneless tuna)

Mix the red wine, juniper berries, orange zest, orange juice, thyme, garlic, pepper and oil. Let stand one day to blend flavors.

Remove skin from tuna steak with a sharp thin knife. The tuna bone forms a cross shape. Insert the point of the knife at center round bone and follow bone to outside edge. Insert knife at center again and follow bone to other edge, removing one steak. Repeat with remaining sections; there will be 4 boneless steaks.

Marinate the steaks in a non-corrosive pan for 3 hours, basting several times. Do not marinate overnight or tuna will become soggy.

Bring tuna to room temperature before grilling. Drain, reserve marinade and pat tuna dry with paper towels. Brush grill with oil and sear tuna over medium high heat for 4 minutes, turning every minute to prevent sticking. Cook tuna for a total of 4 more minutes over medium heat, turning every 2 minutes and basting with warmed marinade. Let steaks stand loosely covered in a warm place for 5 minutes before serving.

Hint: Serve a refreshing cucumber salad with sour cream and fress dill dressing as a refreshing accompaniment. Try the marinade with swordfish.

Serves: 4.

Mediterranean Lamb Shish Kabob

This adaptation of my partner's (Vivian Portner) is a Creative Caterer's classic. Serve with rice pilaf and a crisp Greek salad with feta cheese.

½ cup tomato paste
¼ cup red wine vinegar
½ cup olive oil
4 to 5 cloves garlic, peeled, minced
2 Tablespoons dried oregano
½ teaspoon salt
½ teaspoon freshly ground black pepper
5 pound leg of lamb, sirloin section, boned and cut into 1-inch cubes
2 green peppers, seeded, cut into 1-inch cubes
2 red onions, peeled, quartered and separated
1 pound mushrooms, wiped clean
1 pint box cherry tomatoes
2 Tablespoons olive oil

Whisk the tomato paste, wine vinegar and the ½ cup olive oil together. Stir in the garlic, oregano, salt and pepper. Add the lamb, peppers and onions to the marinade and toss to coat. Cover and refrigerate for 1 to 2 days, stirring occasionally. Add mushrooms to the marinade just before skewering.

Alternate the lamb, peppers, onions and mushrooms on skewers, using 2 skewers and a total of 6 to 8 pieces of meat for each person. To achieve even cooking, do not push food too tightly together. Put the cherry tomatoes on separate skewers, and brush with the two tablespoons olive oil. Assemble skewers one day ahead, if desired.

Bring kabobs to room temperature before cooking. Sear kabobs on high heat for 4 minutes, turning once, and grill on medium high heat for 6 to 10 more minutes, turning every 2 minutes, until lamb is pink in the center. Grill tomatoes for 4 minutes, turning once. Let lamb stand loosely covered in a 175° oven for 5 minutes before serving to let lamb juices flow to the outside of the meat. Remove tomatoes from skewers and pass in a separate bowl.

Serves: 8.

Five Spice Ribs

Oyster sauce is made from oyster extract, water and seasonings and is often used in Cantonese cooking as an alternative to soy sauce; it refrigerates indefinitely after opening. Five spice powder is an Oriental spice blend used to season meat, fish and poultry. It is a combination of fennel seeds, anise, nutmeg, ginger root, cinnamon, cloves, licorice or Sichuan peppercorns. These two items are available in Oriental markets.

> 3 *pounds baby back ribs*
> 3 *Tablespoons oyster sauce*
> 3 *quarter-size slices peeled ginger*
> 2 *garlic cloves, sliced*
> 2 *teaspoons five spice powder*
> 1 *teaspoon cumin*
> 30 *black peppercorns*

Marinade

> ½ *cup oyster sauce*
> 2 *Tablespoons rice vinegar*
> 2 *teaspoons five spice powder*
> 1 *teaspoon cumin*
> 1 *teaspoon black pepper*
> ½ *teaspoon white pepper*
> ¾ *cup honey*
> 3 *quarter-size slices peeled ginger, slivered*

Place ribs in a large pot and cover with cold water. Stir in 3 tablespoons oyster sauce, ginger, garlic, five spice powder, cumin and peppercorns. Bring to a boil, cover and reduce heat, and simmer for 30 minutes. Drain ribs.

To prepare the marinade, mix the oyster sauce, rice vinegar, five spice powder, cumin, black pepper, white pepper, honey and ginger. Pour over ribs, cover and refrigerate 6 hours or overnight.

Bring ribs to room temperature before grilling. Drain ribs and in a small pot, heat marinade. Grill ribs over medium high heat for a total of 8 to 12 minutes, turning and basting with heated marinade every 2 minutes. The ribs should be crisp and shiny when cooked. Cut each rack into individual ribs to serve.

Yield: about 30 ribs or 4 dinner servings.

VEGETABLE MIXED GRILL

Grilled vegetables are a wonderful accompaniment to any meal! In the past, they have often been overlooked or people have limited their selections to vegetables such as tomatoes, peppers and onions. Almost any vegetable with a high water content can be successfully grilled, such as eggplant, corn, mushrooms, potatoes, sweet potatoes, endive and squash (including zucchini, yellow squash, acorn, chayote and pattypan squash). To quickly cook acorn, chayote or pattypan squash, slice crosswise into $1/3$-inch thick large rounds, removing seeds when necessary, and grill.

Vegetables naturally absorb flavor, making them ideal candidates for marinating or cooking over fragrant woods such as mesquite or hickory. Often vegetables are foil wrapped and grilled on the rack or in the coals but I prefer to barbeque vegetables directly on the grill to absorb the smoky flavor. In addition, baste vegetables with marinade and garlic oil before or during cooking to retain moisture and keep skin tender since the intense heat of the barbeque dries the exterior of the vegetable. To retain moisture, avoid peeling vegetables. Sear vegetables over high heat, then move them to the side to finish cooking over lower heat. Turn vegetables for even cooking.

Many grilled vegetables are delicious served at room temperature, If desired, grill vegetables before guests arrive to free the grill for cooking appetizers and the main course.

Cooking Times for Vegetables

Vegetable	Total Cooking Time
eggplant—½-inch slices or wedges	8-12 minutes
corn—in husks, silk removed	15 minutes
mushrooms—whole	10 minutes
potatoes—large, whole, uncooked	45 minutes
large, whole, partly cooked	15-20 minutes
¼-inch slices, uncooked	6-8 minutes
½-inch wedges, uncooked	8-10 minutes
sweet potatoes—halved, partly cooked	15-20 minutes
endive—halved	10 minutes
onions—whole	30 minutes
halved through root end	15-20 minutes
½-inch slices or wedges	10-15 minutes
peppers—1-inch chunks or strips	10 minutes
whole	15-20 minutes
squash—⅓-inch slices	8-10 minutes
tomatoes—cherry or ½-inch slices	3-4 minutes

Turn vegetables every 1-2 minutes for even cooking and to prevent burning.

Garlic New Potatoes

Potatoes and garlic are made for each other. The best potatoes to use for grilling are the dense, firm textured ones such as new, red and boiling potatoes. Small whole and unpeeled potatoes can be cooked directly on the grill. Prick skin before cooking. Larger whole potatoes can be grilled if partly cooked by parboiling or microwaving before grilling. You can turn potatoes into home fries with a crusty exterior and soft and fluffy inside by grilling them as ¼-inch thick slices or ½-inch wide wedges.

> 8 whole new potatoes
> ½ cup garlic oil (page 16)
> ½ to 1 teaspoon Kosher (coarse salt)
> ½ to 1 teaspoon freshly ground coarse black pepper,
>   ground dried chilies, chili powder, minced fresh dill or
>   other fresh herb, to taste

Leave potatoes whole, slice, or cut into wedges. Brush potatoes with the garlic oil, sprinkle them with salt and pepper and grill until crispy, turning and basting often. If desired, stir chilies, chili powder, fresh herbs or other seasonings into the garlic oil before basting.

Potatoes	Cooking Time
Large whole uncooked potatoes	45 minutes total
Large whole partly cooked potatoes	15-20 minutes total
½-inch uncooked potato wedges	8-10 minutes total
¼-inch uncooked potato slices	6-8 minutes total

Serves: 8.

Swedish Potatoes with Fresh Dill

These accordian style potatoes are fun to eat and easy to make. To ease cutting, rest the potatoes between two chopsticks (or clean pencils) and press the chopsticks together against the bottom side of the potato while you slice down without cutting through the potato completely.

> 6 *Tablespoons butter, melted*
> 1 *teaspoon salt*
> ½ *teaspoon freshly ground black pepper*
> 2 *Tablespoons minced fresh dill or other fresh herb*
> 8 *medium boiling potatoes, unpeeled*

In a small bowl combine the butter, salt, pepper and dill. Cut a thin slice from the long side of each potato so that the potato will have a firm base. With a sharp knife make a series of parallel vertical cuts ⅛-inch apart and to within ¼-inch of the base. Be careful not to cut through the base completely.

Cut two squares of heavy foil large enough to wrap 4 potatoes each. Place 4 potatoes on each square, spread the slices gently and brush generously with the butter. Seal each packet with double folds around the edges.

Grill potatoes over medium high heat for 45 minutes, turning every 10 minutes to avoid excessive charring, until a skewer poked gently into the top of a packet slides easily into a potato. Do not turn a packet upside down after this or the butter will run out.

Serves: 8.

Dill

Sweet Potatoes with Madeira Apricot Glaze

Sweet potatoes seem to have a natural affinity for fruit; this apricot and madeira glaze goes perfectly with the potatoes. As an alternative, try the glaze with poultry, pork, shrimp, onions or squash.

   2 *sweet potatoes (10 ounces each)*
   ½ *cup apricot preserves, pureed*
   2 *Tablespoons Madeira*
   2 *garlic cloves, peeled and minced*
   ¼ *teaspoon salt*
   ¼ *teaspoon freshly ground black pepper*

Prick the unpeeled sweet potatoes with a fork and microwave for 5 minutes or bake at 350° for 30 minutes until partly cooked.

Peel potatoes and quarter lengthwise, then halve each quarter crosswise. Mix the apricot preserves and Madeira. Mash the garlic with the salt and pepper to form a paste and stir into the preserves, making about ¾ cup glaze.

Brush the grill well with oil to prevent sticking and grill potatoes over medium high heat for 2 minutes. Brush the grilled surface with the warmed glaze and continue to grill the potatoes for a total of 15 to 20 minutes, turning potatoes and brushing with glaze every 2 minutes until shiny and crisp on the outside.

These potatoes make a good accompaniment to ribs, pork or chicken.

Hint: A wide metal spatula works well for turning the potatoes, since the potatoes will slip off tongs.

Serves: 4.

Lemon Curried Vegetable Kabobs

This tart and hearty marinade complements almost any vegetable that can be grilled. Serve these juicy kabobs with poultry, lamb, pork or beef.

    1 recipe Curry Marinade (recipe follows)
    1 red pepper, seeded, cut into 1-inch chunks
    2 zucchini, sliced into ⅓-inch thick rounds
    2 yellow squash, sliced into ⅓-inch thick rounds
    16 small mushrooms, cleaned
    8 small onions, peeled

Curry Marinade

    3 Tablespoons corn oil
    1 onion, peeled, minced
    2 cloves garlic, minced
    ½ teaspoon minced fresh ginger
    ½ teaspoon salt
    ½ teaspoon turmeric
    ½ teaspoon chili powder
    ½ teaspoon ground cumin
    ¼ teaspoon freshly ground black pepper
    ¼ teaspoon dry mustard
       juice of 1 lemon
    1 Tablespoon tomato paste
    6 Tablespoons plain flavored yogurt
    2 Tablespoons sour cream

To prepare the marinade, heat oil and sauté the onion, garlic, ginger, salt, turmeric, chili powder, cumin, pepper and dry mustard for 3 to 4 minutes on medium low heat. Remove from heat and stir in the lemon juice, tomato paste, yogurt and sour cream.

Stir the vegetables into the cooled curry mixture and marinate for 4 hours. Arrange the vegetables on skewers, alternating ingredients. The kabobs may be assembled one day ahead. Bring to room temperature before cooking.

Grill the kabobs over medium high heat for a total of 10 to 12 minutes, turning every two minutes. Serve hot or at room temperature.

Serves: 4 to 6.

Low Sodium Vegetable Kabobs Monaco

Make the marinade for this recipe at least 2 hours before using to allow the flavors to develop, then marinate vegetables only 1 to 2 hours, or they will become soggy from the acid in the marinade.

⅓ cup dry white wine
¼ cup fresh lime juice
¼ cup fresh lemon juice
¼ cup corn oil
½ teaspoon freshly ground black pepper
1 teaspoon dried tarragon
¼ teaspoon dried rosemary
1 to 2 peeled garlic cloves, minced
1 green pepper, seeded, cut into 1-inch chunks
1 red or yellow pepper, cut into 1-inch chunks
1 large red onion, peeled and cut into 8 wedges
2 zucchini (or other squash) cut into ½-inch circles
32 mushrooms (about 1 ½ pounds)
32 cherry tomatoes
1 teaspoon salt (optional)

In a large bowl, mix the wine, lime juice, lemon juice, oil, pepper, tarragon, rosemary and garlic either two hours before using or one day ahead. Add the peppers, onion, zucchini and mushrooms and marinate 1 to 2 hours, stirring occasionally.

Drain the vegetables and add the tomatoes to the marinade. Thread the vegetables onto 16 skewers, alternating ingredients. Drain tomatoes, reserve the marinade and thread tomatoes onto separate skewers since their cooking time is so short. Sprinkle kabobs with salt just before grilling if desired.

Brush grill with oil, and grill kabobs over medium high heat for a total of 10-12 minutes, turning every 2 minutes, and basting with the warmed marinade. Grill tomatoes for 3 minutes, then remove from skewers and pass separately.

Hint: The Monaco Marinade is also excellent with poultry, veal, fish or seafood.

Serves: 8.

Grilled Herbed French Bread

We heat hamburger and hot dog buns all the time on the grill but rarely use other breads. While you have the grill heated to cook a meal, use it to toast thick slices of French bread, jalapeño corn bread, pita wedges, bagels and corn or flour tortillas. Grill breads "as is" or brush with plain melted butter or with herb and spice-flecked butter to match the mood of your meal.

1 *loaf French bread*
¼ *cup melted butter*
¼ *cup garlic oil (page 16)*
  minced fresh herbs or spices to taste
½ *cup grated Parmesan cheese (optional)*

Cut the bread into ½ to 1-inch thick diagonal slices. Cut slices in half crosswise if they are too large. Mix equal portions of melted butter and garlic oil with fresh or dried herbs such as basil, oregano, marjoram, thyme, tarragon, rosemary, parsley or dill.

Brush bread lightly with herb butter and grill over medium low heat until crispy and brown. If desired, sprinkle with grated Parmesan cheese 2 to 3 minutes before removing from grill.

Variations: Fragrant oils such as sesame, Oriental chili, walnut, almond, hazelnut or avocado can replace the garlic oil, but use in smaller proportions than the garlic oil.

Try spices such as cumin, chili powder, ground roasted Sichuan peppercorns, paprika, cayenne, mustard, turmeric, or any ground dried chili peppers for added zest!

For crunch, add poppy, sesame, celery or caraway seeds; for flavor, fresh lemon juice, Tabasco®, Worcestershire sauce, tomato paste, Ao Nori (dried seaweed flakes), or soy sauce.

Yield: 25 slices.

THEME PARTIES

Middle Eastern Barbeque

Miniature Kefta with Mint Chutney *
Marinated Black and Green Olives
Butterflied Leg of Lamb *
Mediterranean Vegetable Medley *
Pita Bread Wedges
Couscous and Feta Salad *
Baklava
Turkish Coffee

(Recipes Provided)*

Miniature Kefta with Mint Chutney

These bite size kabobs are highly seasoned with traditional spices and refreshing herbs. Form the lamb into larger and longer cigar shapes for an entrée or into patties to eat in plump warm pita halves. Serve with a robust mint chutney.

- 1 pound ground lamb
- ¼ cup finely chopped white onion
- 2 teaspoons cumin
- 2 Tablespoons minced fresh parsley
- 1 Tablespoon minced fresh mint
- 1 teaspoon Sambal Oelek (ground chili paste) *
- 1 teaspoon minced garlic
- ½ teaspoon salt
- ½ teaspoon white pepper
- ¼ teaspoon ground black pepper

Mint Chutney

   6 Tablespoons minced fresh mint or 2 to 3 Tablespoons
      dried mint
   2 Tablespoons minced white onion
   3 Tablespoons lemon juice
   1 Tablespoon white vinegar
   3 Tablespoons water
   ¾ teaspoon salt
   ¼ to ½ teaspoon Sambel Oelek (ground chili paste) *
   * Sambal Oelek is made from ground fresh chilies, vinegar
      and salt and is available in Oriental markets.

In a medium-sized bowl, mix the lamb, onion, cumin, parsley, mint, Sambel Oelek, garlic, salt, white pepper and black pepper. Let stand for one hour to blend flavors.

Set aside sixteen 6 or 8-inch bamboo skewers. To assemble the kabobs, grasp enough lamb to make a ball about half the size of an egg and divide ball in two. Hold the meat in the left hand, place skewer on the meat and squeeze fingers around the lamb to encircle the skewer. Shape the meat into a cigar shape about 1½-inches long. Repeat with a second ball near the point of the same skewer, leaving 2 inches between each piece of meat. Assemble remaining skewers in the same fashion. Cover with plastic wrap and refrigerate one day in advance if desired.

To prepare the mint chutney, in a small bowl mix the mint, onion, lemon juice, vinegar, water, salt and Sambel Oelek. Let stand one hour before serving.

Lightly brush grill with oil before using. Grill the kefta over a hot fire for a total of 6 to 8 minutes, turning every 2 minutes until medium rare. Serve immediately or keep warm, loosely covered in a 175° oven.

Arrange the kefta on a brass tray with the mint chutney in a small bowl in the center. Serve the kefta on small plates and spoon chutney onto them.

Hint: The mint chutney is an excellent accompaniment to pork, firm-fleshed white fish and seafood. Substitute fresh cilantro for the mint for an exciting variation.

Serves: 8 appetizer portions.

Butterflied Leg of Lamb

A boned leg of lamb is fun to barbeque. It will be a unique experience for many of your guests. Fresh rosemary is my favorite herb with this marinade; if not available use fresh dill in its place for equally delicious results.

   4 *large cloves garlic, peeled and finely chopped*
   4 *Tablespoons chopped fresh rosemary, dill or parsley*
   1 *cup dry red wine*
   2 *Tablespoons red wine vinegar*
   5 *Tablespoons olive oil*
   1 *teaspoon olive oil*
   1 *teaspoon freshly ground black pepper*
   5 *pound leg of lamb, sirloin section, trimmed, boned and butterflied*

In a rectangular glass pan, mix the garlic, rosemary, red wine, red wine vinegar, olive oil and black pepper together. Place the lamb in the pan and baste with the marinade. Cover and refrigerate overnight, basting and turning occasionally.

Bring lamb to room temperature before grilling. Place the lamb flat on a lightly oiled barbeque rack and cook over medium high heat 10 to 14 minutes per side until rare. Heat the marinade and baste the lamb with marinade. Turn lamb several times.

There will be thin and thick portions to the lamb. Cut those pieces from the leg as they are cooked to the rare stage, and place the meat on a pre-heated platter. Loosely cover the lamb with foil and let rest in a warm place or 175° oven for 10 minutes to allow the meat juices to redistribute throughout the leg. Slice lamb across the grain and serve with the accumulated pan juices.

Note: Sirloin section is a leg of lamb with the lower shank or thin bony end of the leg removed. Your butcher will usually bone lamb at no extra charge, but it is easy to do yourself. Remove all exterior fat first from the leg. Using a very sharp small bladed knife, place the blade flat against the bone and cut the meat away with short quick strokes. Follow the bone through the leg and remove. Slash very thick parts of the leg so it will lie flat on the grill.

Serves: 8.

Mediterranean Vegetable Medley

These succulent and fragrant grilled vegetables are excellent served with lamb, steak or hamburgers. If desired, cut thinly sliced Provolone or Kasseri cheese to fit the vegetable slices and place the cheese on top of vegetables during the last two minutes of cooking until melted.

1½ pounds eggplant
 1 to 2 teaspoons salt
1½ pounds medium yellow squash
1½ pounds medium zucchini
 ¾ cup garlic oil (page 16)
1½ Tablespoon dried oregano leaves or 3 Tablespoons
     minced fresh oregano
1½ Tablespoons dried marjoram leaves or 3 Tablespoons
     minced fresh marjoram
 1 to 2 Tablespoons Kosher (coarse) salt
 ½ to 1 Tablespoon freshly ground black pepper

To prepare the vegetables, wipe the eggplant, remove stem end and slice lengthwise into ½-inch steaks. If using Italian or Oriental eggplant (long, thin eggplants), cut in half lengthwise. Sprinkle eggplant with 1 to 2 teaspoons salt, cover with plastic wrap and place a heavy weight on top to force out any bitter juices. Let stand at room temperature for 40 to 50 minutes. Drain accumulated juices, and wipe cut surfaces of eggplant dry.

Slice yellow squash and zucchini lengthwise into ½-inch steaks. Lay eggplant, yellow squash and zucchini on a cookie sheet and brush top with garlic oil. Mix oregano and marjoram. Rub a small quantity of dried herb mixture between the heels of the hand to release flavor. Sprinkle herbs on top of vegetables along with the coarsely ground salt and pepper. Turn slices over and repeat all steps on the second side. Make a second layer with remaining vegetables and repeat sprinkling with herbs.

Brush grill with oil and place eggplant, yellow squash and zucchini directly on grill in single layers over medium high heat for a total of 8 minutes, turning every 2 minutes. Brush vegetables with remaining garlic oil as they cook.

Serve warm or at room temperature.

Serves: 8.

Couscous and Feta Salad

To fully appreciate the refreshing flavors and variety of textures that are featured here—crisp red radish slices, slightly chewy couscous, crunchy pistachio nuts and tender cubes of feta cheese—serve this salad as a separate course.

 7 *Tablespoons white wine vinegar*
 3 *Tablespoons fresh lemon juice*
 6 *Tablespoons peanut oil*
 1 *Tablespoon Kosher (coarse) salt*
 1 *Tablespoon freshly ground black pepper*
 ½ *cup water*
 1 *cup couscous (available in most supermarkets)*
 4 *green onions, minced*
 1 *cucumber, seeded, cubed into ½-inch dice*
 1 *cup chopped fresh mint or 2 to 3 Tablespoons crushed dried mint*
 4 *ounces feta cheese, cut into ½-inch cubes*
 12 *radishes, very thinly sliced*
 1 *cup shelled pistachios*

To prepare the dressing, in a small bowl, whisk 3 tablespoons of the vinegar with the lemon juice, peanut oil, 2 teaspoons of the salt and pepper. The dressing is very strong since the couscous and vegetables dilute it.

In a medium-size saucepan, bring the water, 4 tablespoons of the white wine vinegar and 1 teaspoon of the salt to a boil. Remove from the heat and quickly stir in the couscous. Cover and let stand off the heat for 5 minutes until the couscous swells. The couscous should be chewy but soft enough to bite into. Stir with a chopstick or fork to fluff grains. This makes about 3 cups.

In a large bowl, toss the warm couscous with the green onions, cucumber, mint and feta cheese. Whisk the dressing and pour over the salad. Toss, taste for seasonings and let stand at room temperature for 1 hour. Add the radishes and pistachios just before serving to prevent radish color from bleeding and nuts from getting soft.

Serve salad at room temperature in a large glass bowl or dark blue ceramic dish.

Serves: 8 dinner portions.

Sleepy Appetites Meet The Breakfast Cookout

Fresh Bagels
Scallion Cream Cheese
Smoked Nova Scotia Salmon
Grilled Bacon & Sausages *
Herbed Scrambled Eggs with Cheese *
Grilled Green Tomatoes *
Hot English Mustard *
Country Ham * *with Miniature Cornbread Muffins*
Honey Wheat English Muffins
Strawberry Preserves
Honeydew Melon with Fresh Lemon
Ripe Red Cherries
Coffee

(* Recipes Provided)

(Feeds 4 Hungry People)

Even scrambled eggs taste better cooked on the grill. Back home in Canada's Ottowa Valley, we often invite friends over to enjoy a leisurely brunch on a sunny Sunday morning.

While the rest of the food is cooking, stave off hunger pangs with bagels and smoked fish. Toast the bagels and spread with speckled scallion cream cheese. Top with slices of coral-pink smoked salmon. Count on one bagel per person and one quarter pound of smoked salmon for the group.

Start cooking the bacon and sausages first and while they're on the grill, you'll have plenty of time to prepare the tomatoes, scrambled eggs and fruit. The high-fat foods need a drip pan underneath while cooking. It is easy to fashion a griddle by placing a cake-cooling rack on top of two disposable foil pans— with a lip to hold in the fat, disposable for easy clean-up and two pans for support.

Serve a zesty homemade English mustard with the meal. Extend the British theme for a mixed grill with tenderloin lamb chops, bacon wrapped kidneys or small beef tenderloin. Or, add a European touch instead with mild German knockwurst or spicy Spanish chorizo. These sausages can be cooked directly on the grill to heat them through.

Green tomatoes have a wonderful piquant flavor to complement the smoky country ham or Canadian back bacon. Serve warm cornbread muffins and toasted English muffins and finish the meal with refreshing melon and ripe cherries.

Grilled Bacon and Sausages

½ pound bacon
½ pound small pork sausage

Cut the bacon strips in half and prick sausages with a fork to release fat while cooking. Lay bacon and sausages on griddle and cook over high heat with cover of grill closed for 15 to 20 minutes, turning once. Drain fat during cooking with a metal baster, leaving 1 to 2 tablespoons of drippings for grilling tomatoes. Remove bacon and sausages and keep warm.

Note: If your grill doesn't have a cover, you'll need to cook bacon and sausages a few minutes longer.

Herb Scrambled Eggs with Cheese

    8 eggs
    ½ cup cold water
    1 ounce blue cheese, crumbled
    2 Tablespoons minced fresh chives
    1 ounce sharp cheddar cheese, crumbled
    2 Tablespoons minced fresh basil or 2 teaspoons dried
       basil
       salt and pepper to taste

Grease the bottom and sides of two 8-inch x 7-inch foil pans or spray with vegetable oil. In one pan, whisk 4 eggs, ¼ cup water, blue cheese and chives together; in the second pan, repeat with the remaining eggs, water, cheddar cheese and basil. Season with salt and pepper.

Cook eggs on medium heat with grill cover down for 4 to 6 minutes, stirring occasionally. Do not overcook or cheese will become tough and stringy. Serve warm.

Note: If your grill doesn't have a cover, the eggs will take slightly longer to cook.

Grilled Green Tomatoes

    ¼ cup flour
    2 teaspoons brown sugar
    2 Tablespoons minced fresh basil or 2 teaspoons dried
       basil
    ½ teaspoon salt
    ¼ teaspoon freshly ground black pepper
    4 large green tomatoes, sliced crosswise ½-inch thick
    1 to 2 Tablespoons bacon drippings

In a small bowl mix the flour, sugar, basil, salt and pepper. Coat both sides of the tomato slices generously with the flour mixture. Heat drippings in griddle until very hot and grill the tomatoes on the griddle for 4 to 6 minutes until crisp and brown, turning once.

Hot English Mustard

 2 Tablespoons dry mustard
 1½ Tablespoons sugar
 1 Tablespoon plus 2 teaspoons flour
 2 Tablespoons cider vinegar

In a bowl, mix the mustard, sugar and flour together. Stir in the vinegar to form a smooth paste. The mustard should be thick enough to just fall off the end of a spoon. Let the mustard stand for 15 minutes to develop flavor. Store tightly covered at room temperature.

Country Ham

 1 boneless country ham slice (7 to 8 ounces) or 7 to 8
   ounces Canadian back bacon, sliced ¼-inch thick

Trim fat from ham. Grill ham or bacon over medium heat for 3 to 4 minutes, turning once. Do not overcook or ham will dry out.

Mustard

Stuck On Kabobs

Assorted Kabobs—
*Beef, Chicken, Lamb, Pork, Fish, Seafood & Vegetables **
*Crusty French Bread with Herb Cheese **
*Million Dollar Summer Salad **
*Baked Potatoes with Dill Sauce **
Seasonal Fresh Fruit
Coolers

(* Recipes Provided)

A picnic with 12 to 15 friends allows for lots of variety. Pick your favorite spot for a day of sun, sport and good eating, and share in bringing the cooking gear, sports equipment and food. Friends who love to eat, but whose kitchen skills are less than adequate can bring skewers, paper goods, glasses, wood chips, charcoal and ice. For a day long outing, allow 2 to 3 napkins and glasses and at least one pound of ice per person. This provides enough ice for both icing down and putting into beverages. Remember to include ice chests and coolers to combat the hot weather. All of the recipes provided can be prepared at home and transported to the picnic for grilling or eating.

Assorted Kabobs

Everyone loves skewered food, and it is fun to have a variety of meat, poultry, fish and vegetables for each person to make their own kabobs. See chart on page 61 for cooking times for various kabobs. Pair foods with similar cooking times.

Companions—Potatoes, Crusty French Bread, Salad, Dessert

Grill potatoes whole or in a variety of ways (page 44) and use French bread, rye rounds, pumpernickel or other breads with the creamy herb cheese (recipe follows). Pick salads that are worry free and will not wilt or spoil in humid hot summer weather. The Million Dollar Summer Salad is easily adapted by varying the herbs and produce—try red, green or yellow peppers, or blanched yellow squash, asparagus or fresh beets. For dessert, pile chunks of cantaloupe, honeydew, watermelon, peaches and raspberries into individual 9-ounce disposable glasses and marinate in a combination of Moselle wine and an inexpensive champagne.

Sauces

Bring your favorite barbeque sauce, a topping for the baked potatoes, or an herb spread or garlic butter for the bread. Fresh vegetables with a cool dipping sauce are great to have on hand to tide people over until the serious cooking and eating begin.

Coolers

Include lots of refreshing drinks. Choose from lemonade, beer, wine, soda or cooling juices.

Make Your Own Kabobs

The key to successful cooking is to group foods on the same skewer that take about the same amount of time to cook: for example, chicken and squash; beef, lamb and zucchini; pork and peppers. Sprinkle toasted sesame seeds on meat for extra flavor and crunch; choose firm-fleshed fish that will retain its shape. Use 5-inch bamboo skewers for appetizers and 8 to 10-inch skewers for the main course. See the chart below for specific cooking times and sizes of food for making kabobs. Other kabob recipes can be found on pages 35, 36, 38, 40, 47, 48, and 50.

Great Kabob Foods

Meat, Poulty, Fish, Shellfish and Vegetables
Pair Foods with Similar Cooking Times

SIZE	COOKING TIME PER SIDE				
	1-2 Min.	2-3 Min.	3-5 Min.	5-6 Min.	7-8 Min.
1-inch Cubes					
Rare Beef & Lamb			★		
Pork					★
Chicken				★	
Fish			★		
1-inch Squares					
Peppers & Onions				★	
⅛-inch slices					
Zucchini & Yellow Squash				★	
Strips: ⅛-inch thick, 1-inch wide, 3-inches long					
Beef & Lamb		★			
Pork & Chicken			★		
Other					
Shrimp & Scallops			★		
Cherry Tomatoes	★				
Mushrooms			★		

Crusty French Bread with Herb Cheese

> 4 ounces blue cheese, room temperature
> 12 ounces cream cheese, cubed, room temperature
> ¼ cup minced fresh parsley
> ¼ cup minced fresh chives or shallots
> 2 teaspoons minced garlic
> ½ teaspoon salt
> 8 to 10 drops Tabasco®
> 2 loaves French bread, sliced thick, diagonally

In the bowl of an electric mixer, cream the blue cheese until smooth. Gradually mix in the cream cheese, parsley, chives, garlic, salt and Tabasco. Taste and adjust seasonings.

Grill French bread for 10 to 20 seconds, and serve warm, spread with softened herb cheese.

Serves: 16.

Million Dollar Summer Salad

> 1 recipe Sherry Vinaigrette (recipe follows)
> 1 pound green beans
> 1 pound yellow beans
> 1 cucumber
> 2 tomatoes

Sherry Vinaigrette
> ¼ cup sherry vinegar, red wine, balsamic or tarragon vinegar
> 1 teaspoon salt
> 3 large garlic cloves, minced
> ¾ cup peanut oil
> ½ teaspoon freshly ground black pepper
> ¼ teaspoon white pepper
> 2 Tablespoons minced fresh tarragon or 2 teaspoons dried tarragon
> 2 Tablespoons minced fresh parsley or tarragon (optional—for garnish)

To prepare the vinaigrette, in a bowl, whisk the vinegar, salt, garlic, peanut oil, black and white pepper and 2 tablespoons tarragon together. Taste and adjust seasonings. The dressing should be quite strong since the vegetables will dilute it.

Wash the beans, remove stem ends and leave beans whole. Steam beans in separate pots for 3 to 5 minutes each or until tender-crisp. Immerse beans in cold water to stop cooking and dry beans in layers on clean dish towels. Prepare one day ahead if desired and refrigerate loosely wrapped in paper towels in a plastic bag.

Peel cucumber lengthwise, leaving four thin strips of peel for color. Cut cucumber in half lengthwise, remove seeds with a melon baller and diagonally cut cucumber into 15 to 20 slices per half. Keep slices together and store refrigerated on several layers of paper towels wrapped in plastic wrap.

Core tomatoes and half lengthwise. Place the cut side down and slice each half into 10 slices. Repeat cucumber storage technique.

Two hours before serving, toss the beans separately with just enough dressing to lightly coat. Place the beans on either end of a platter with rows of tomatoes and cucumbers in between. Drizzle the cucumbers and tomatoes with dressing and sprinkle with minced fresh parsley or tarragon, if desired.

Serves: 8.

Chives

Baked Potatoes with Dill Sauce

16 medium Red Bliss, new or boiling potatoes
½ cup melted butter
    Kosher (coarse) salt to taste
    freshly ground black pepper to taste

Dill Sauce
2 cups sour cream
2 teaspoons dry mustard
1 cup plain flavored yogurt
½ cup minced fresh dill
½ teaspoon salt

To prepare the sauce, in a bowl, mix a bit of the sour cream with the mustard to form a paste. Stir in the remaining sour cream, yogurt, dill and salt. Taste and adjust seasonings. Refrigerate.

Wipe potatoes clean, dry, and prick skin with a fork. You will need enough heavy duty foil to wrap 4 packages of 4 potatoes each. Place the potatoes on the foil, brush the skins with melted butter and generously sprinkle with salt and pepper. Wrap potatoes, folding top and sides of foil over twice to seal.

Grill potatoes over high heat for 40 to 50 minutes, turning every 15 minutes. Test doneness by inserting a toothpick through the foil and into the potato. Do not invert package once potatoes have been tested, or the butter will run out. Serve with dill sauce.
Serves: 16.

Dill